KNOWLEDGE ENCYCLOPEDIA

RENAISSANCE ARCHITECTURE

© Wonder House Books 2021

All rights reserved. No part of this book may be reproduced or transmitted in any form by any means, electronic or mechanical, including photocopying and recording, or by any information storage and retrieval system except as may be expressly permitted in writing by the publisher.

(An imprint of Prakash Books)

contact@wonderhousebooks.com

Disclaimer: The information contained in this encyclopedia has been collated with inputs from subject experts. All information contained herein is true to the best of the Publisher's knowledge.

ISBN : 9789390391646

Table of Contents

Buildings of the Renaissance	3
Identifying Renaissance Architecture	4–5
Early Renaissance in Florence	6–7
Domes on the Skyline	8–9
A Patrician's Home is His Palazzo	10–11
A Vista of Villas	12–13
Secular Architecture	14–15
Boboli Gardens	16–17
Religious Architecture	18–19
The Spread of Renaissance	20–21
Renaissance Architecture in France	22–23
Dutch and Flemish Renaissance	24–25
The Iberian Peninsula	26–27
El Escorial	28–29
The British Isles	30–31
Word Check	32

BUILDINGS OF THE RENAISSANCE

Beginning from the 14th century, architects in the Italian states began to revive Classical Roman and Greek designs for buildings. The new designs became part of the period called the **Renaissance**. Classicism stressed the importance of harmony, symmetry and proportion in all structures, whether a single building or an entire city. The earliest masters of the Renaissance period, like Filippo Brunelleschi, rose in Florence. He was an architect and an engineer. Some of his constructions used machines that he had invented himself. During the **High Renaissance**, the focus shifted to Rome and to geniuses like Donato Bramante, an architect who served as the chief architect for the construction of St Peter's Basilica. During the 15th and 16th centuries, Renaissance spread to the rest of Europe. Here, it combined with native styles to produce entirely unique buildings.

▼ The Duomo di Firenze (Cathedral of Florence) is famous for its Renaissance dome. It was built by the architect Filippo Brunelleschi who invented new ways of engineering to make such a construction possible

Identifying Renaissance Architecture

Renaissance architecture was inspired by Classical notions of order. This can be seen in the geometrical layouts of buildings. Rows of columns and round arches were often repeated in tiers. Proportions (its size and symmetry) were designed according to certain Classical and mathematical formulae. They matched human proportions, the Renaissance ideal of beauty and harmony. Renaissance architects also looked to ancient Roman architects like Vitruvius to guide them in designing the ideal building.

▲ Designed by early Renaissance master Leon Battista Alberti, the amazing facade of the Basilica of Sant'Andrea in Mantua reflects Classical Roman grandeur

▲ The Palazzo Mellini-Fossi of Florence is unusual for having frescoes on the outside rather than its interior. This Renaissance building is painted with scenes from Roman mythology

▲ The Baptistery of Florence is an early revival of Classical symmetry; the blind arches are typical of Renaissance decoration

Renaissance Motifs

Architects of the Renaissance rejected the ornate designs of the earlier Gothic period. On the outside, buildings were relatively flat and plain. Their beauty came from the marble or stone used in construction and from the repetitions of set geometrical patterns. Ancient motifs seen here included blind arches, medallions and three types of Classical columns—Doric, Ionic and Corinthian. Statues were used to decorate nooks and rooftops.

The most easily recognisable order of architecture, Doric is characterised by columns topped by plain circular capitals. The Ionic column is topped by two pairs of volutes. This is a spiral, scroll-like ornament for the pillar. Ionic columns are usually slender and were considered 'female' during Renaissance times. The most complex decoration of columns is called Corinthian. It is seen both on the facades of and inside buildings, where it adds vigour to otherwise strictly Classical lines. The Corinthian pillars end in unfurling leaf- and fern-like motifs. Later, composite columns were created, combining Corinthian columns with Doric or Ionic orders to give designs that were even more ornate.

▲ This Renaissance Puerta del Puente (Gate of the Bridge) has a central square passage with sturdy Doric columns on either side

▶ Corinthian columns at the Cathedral of Pisa

▲ The volutes atop Ionic columns at Palazzo Valmarana

Sansovino's Biblioteca

Jacopo Sansovino (1486–1570) brought the High Renaissance style of architecture to Venice. The library that he designed at Piazza San Marco (St Mark's Square) features regular **bays** in endlessly repeating rows. The space between the arches is decorated with Classical figures and motifs. On the rooftop are tall, elegant statues that offer a vertical contrast to the long building.

▶ *Sansovino's Biblioteca Marciana inspired many later Renaissance architects*

Urban Planning

Renaissance architecture went hand in hand with town planning. It first began with Florence. Unlike other towns of the 15th century, Florence was not dominated by cathedral spires rising above smaller houses and churches. Instead, it was planned to radiate away from the centre in the shape of a star. This model was considered the Classical ideal and was much imitated. The buildings on each street were well defined and created according to harmonious proportions.

▲ *The Ideal City, painted c. 1480–1484, shows the ideal Renaissance town with its triumphant archway, Roman colosseum and octagonal baptistery surrounded by dignified homes. The entire space is broken up according to mathematical principles and reflects a harmony of proportions*

Old Town of Urbino

The hill town of Urbino was a flourishing centre of Renaissance in the 15th century. Under the patronage of its military leader Federico da Montefeltro (1422–1482), the city became a centre for the arts. The architects who were attracted to the city built it according to Renaissance traditions. The University of Urbino, set up in 1506, still operates today. However, from the 16th century onwards, the town's culture and economy began to decline. It has thus preserved its Renaissance appearance and is now a UNESCO World Heritage Site.

▶ *The historic centre of Urbino*

Early Renaissance in Florence

Florence began as an ancient Roman garrison town. During the Renaissance, however, it transformed into a prosperous town of merchants and scholars. The artists and architects who flocked here transformed the city with fine Classical buildings and sculptures.

▶ *The facade of Santa Maria Novella, completed in 1470 by influential architect Leon Battista Alberti, in a mix of Gothic and Renaissance styles*

Baptistery Doors

The eastern doors of the Baptistery of San Giovanni are part of Renaissance legend. Created by Lorenzo Ghiberti (1378–1455), the doors are so extraordinary, Michelangelo named them the 'Gates of Paradise'. They are about 17 feet tall. Each side is divided into five square panels, bearing stories in **relief** from the Old Testament. Inspiration for the figures came from ancient Roman sarcophagus reliefs. The frame of each door is ornamented with statuettes and **roundels**. At the very top and bottom, the frames bear reclining figures.

▶ *The Gates of Paradise at the Florence Baptistery*

The Gates of Paradise

Ghiberti won the commission to create the doors by beating out amazing competition such as architect Filippo Brunelleschi and sculptor Niccolo d'Arezzo. It took ten years to complete just the door panels. Work on the frames ran on till the 1440s. Finally, in 1452, the gilding of the doors was completed. The doors were fixed at the Baptistery's eastern entrance. Ghiberti died three years later.

▲ *This door panel shows God creating the universe, the Garden of Eden and the first humans*

▲ *The panel depicting the life of Joshua, who led the Israelites after the death of Moses*

▲ *One of the roundels bears a self-portrait of Ghiberti*

RENAISSANCE ARCHITECTURE

Pazzi Chapel

One of Filippo Brunelleschi's masterpieces, the Pazzi Chapel follows a circle-and-square design. The atrium, which is a kind of entrance hall, is held up by six Corinthian columns. Inside, the square room lies below an umbrella-shaped dome, bearing round sculptures and the Pazzi coat-of-arms. The walls carry glazed terracotta decorations by Luca della Robbia. The vault over the **apse** is frescoed to reflect the sky over Florence on 4 July 1442.

In Real Life

In 1478, Jacopo and Francesco de Pazzi ambushed their rivals in the Medici family and murdered one of them. The Pazzis paid dearly for their crime. They were exiled and all their lands were confiscated. As a result, the Pazzi Chapel you see today is left still unfinished.

▶ A 1479 drawing of a hanged Pazzi conspirator by Leonardo da Vinci

▲ Luca della Robbia's decorations inside the Pazzi Chapel, with the sky-dome beyond the arch

Palazzo Medici-Riccardi

Around 1444, Cosimo de' Medici hired the architect Michelozzo to build him a home. This became Florence's first Renaissance palatial townhouse. From outside, it is as stern and formidable as a fortress. The rows of arched windows and asymmetrical doors offer little relief. In 1517, the ground floor was altered by adding two 'kneeling windows' designed by Michelangelo. The internal courtyard is a far gentler space. It lies between arched colonnades. A staircase leads to the various quarters and their amazing frescoes.

▲ Michelangelo's 'kneeling window' (finestre inginocchiate) at the Palazzo Medici-Riccardi

▲ The inner courtyard is decorated with the statue of Greek mythological hero Orpheus at the far end

Palazzo Strozzi

The Strozzi family were rivals of the Medicis in Florence. The Palazzo Strozzi was thus purposely designed to be bigger and better than the Palazzo Medici-Riccardi. Work began in 1489 using a design by Benedetto da Maiano. But later, the architect Simone del Pollaiolo took over. This is yet another fortress-like residence. It is built in a rectangle and occupies three floors. A symmetrical structure, it is made of massive stone blocks. Wrought-iron decorations such as torch-holders and flag-holders adorn the facade. The courtyard is surrounded by a stone arcade.

▶ At Palazzo Strozzi, wrought-iron decorations in the shapes of a sphinx and dragon created by the 15th-century blacksmith Niccolò Grosso

Domes on the Skyline

Domed roofs have been around since ancient times. But it was only in Roman times that they became technical marvels. Ancient Roman architects developed engineering principles to build impressive domes. Their knowledge was revived and further developed during the Renaissance. The dome became an architectural wonder. It crowned the most important, most imposing buildings of the Renaissance.

◀ *The double domes of Santa Maria della Salute, on the Grand Canal of Venice, evolved from the revival and further development of ancient Roman styles and engineering. The church was built to thank God for saving the city from the devastating plague outbreak of 1630*

An Architectural Challenge

Domes exert all their pressure outwards along the boundary and can easily collapse. Renaissance builders who planned ambitious domes came up with ways to reduce the weight and pressure of the stone. For instance, they used a system of ribs to support the structure during construction. Such techniques allowed for great variation in the curve and high, awe-inspiring drums. Many domes even had a second, lighter shell on the inside that made the outside and the inside look very different.

The Duomo

The amazing dome of the Cathedral Santa Maria del Fiore began an architectural revolution. This cathedral in Florence is also known as the Duomo. Ilts construction began in 1296. In 1418, a competition was held to decide who would construct the dome for the cathedral. It was to be almost 150 feet wide, a very difficult feat. After much discussion, Filippo Brunelleschi finally won in 1420. The work on the dome began the same year and finally concluded in 1436.

▲ *The dome at Prato's Santa Maria delle Carceri, designed by architect Giuliano da Sangallo, was inspired by Brunelleschi's work. While the inside is a perfect half-sphere, the outside is a combination of cylindrical and conical shapes*

⭐ Incredible Individuals

A talented architect, Filippo Brunelleschi (1377–1446) presented keen technical knowledge and amazing innovations, which marked the beginning of Renaissance architecture. The Duomo, his masterpiece, is the first octagonal dome in history. Brunelleschi designed it with a lantern crowning the top and tribunes (semicircular structures) down the side. He even invented the machines that helped construct the dome! Brunelleschi became the *capomaestro* (chief architect) from 1420 until his death in 1446.

▲ *Florence's Duomo seen from Michelangelo Hill*

RENAISSANCE ARCHITECTURE

Brunelleschi's Dome

Brunelleschi began constructing the dome by first building a tall drum, that is, a cylindrical base. His revolutionary bit of engineering called for a double-shelled dome of brick and stone. Using a wooden frame, the brickwork was placed in a herringbone pattern between stone beams. The octagonal outer shell grew into a pointed arch, supported by ribs. At the very top was an opening topped by a lantern. The inner and outer shells of the dome were held together by a system of arches. In the end, this unit was a freestanding dome requiring no external support!

▶ Giorgio Vasari and Federico Zuccaro painted the inside of Brunelleschi's dome with frescoes of the Last Judgement

St Peter's Basilica

Brilliant architects like Bramante, Raphael and Antonio da Sangallo helped build St Peter's Basilica in Vatican City. Its dome (42 metre in diameter) was designed by Michelangelo using Brunelleschi's methods. It had two shells of wood and stone. When Michelangelo passed away in 1564, Giacomo della Porta completed the work using Michelangelo's basic design. This was a segmented dome with regularly spaced openings. The whole structure rested on a high drum, which had its own windows between paired columns. At the top was a tall and exquisite lantern. Della Porta made the dome higher, gave it more segments and changed the shape of the openings.

▲ The inner dome of St Peter's Basilica, Vatican City

▶ The amazing High Renaissance dome at St Peter's Basilica

A Patrician's Home is His Palazzo

In Renaissance Italy, grand city homes were called palazzi (palazzo in singular). These were not always owned by noblemen. In fact, most palazzi belonged to wealthy **burghers** and clergymen. In general, they were sturdy, rectangular buildings that rose to three or more floors. They had formidable exteriors built to Classical proportions. Later in the Renaissance period, the buildings became more ornate.

▲ The late-Renaissance Palazzo Chiericati, designed by Andrea Palladio, has a more ornamental facade but still follows Classical principles in its construction

▲ Palazzo Marino, an ambitious High Renaissance townhouse designed by Galeazzo Alessi for the powerful banker Tommaso Marino. It is now Milan's city hall

Palazzo Interiors

Sumptuous courtyards and walled gardens lay inside a palazzo, decorated with brilliant sculptures and fragrant plants. The rooms were vibrantly frescoed by the masters of the period.

▲ The amazing Sala dei Fasti Farnesiani (Room of Farnese Deeds) at Villa Farnese is the work of brothers Taddeo and Federico Zuccaro. They depicted the glorious history of the Farnese family

Villa Farnese

The Villa Farnese dominates the town of Caprarola. It is an amazing Renaissance and Mannerist building that overlooks the hills of Monti Cimini. The palazzo is built in the form of a pentagon in reddish-gold stone. Antonio da Sangallo the Younger (1484–1546), a brilliant military engineer, originally designed it as a five-sided fortress. In the mid 16th century, architect Giacomo Barozzi da Vignola (1507–1573) took over. He kept the shape but created a grand palazzo with hundreds of rooms and a beautiful garden.

▼ An example of Renaissance architecture, Villa Farnese is large and built using harmonious proportions, but is sparingly ornamented

RENAISSANCE ARCHITECTURE

 ## Royal Stairs

Supported by Ionic columns, Villa Farnese's galleried court is ornamented with busts of the Roman emperors. Five spiral staircases lead to the upper floors. The most magnificent of these is a graceful spiral of steps called the *Scala Regia* (Royal Stairs). It is held up by Ionic pillars and rises up three magnificent floors.

▲ The upper landing of the Scala Regia

▲ View of the dome from the Scala Regia

 ## Hall of Hercules

Each of the five floors at Villa Farnese has a different purpose. The main rooms are on the *piano nobile* (first floor). Here, a central **loggia** looks down over the town. This hall is called the Sala d'Ercole (Hall of Hercules), after its mythological frescoes done by Federico Zuccaro (c. 1541–1609). At one end is a grotto-like fountain with statues.

▶ The fountain in the Hall of Hercules

 ## Palazzo del Te

The summer palace of Duke Federico Gonzaga II, Palazzo del Te was built over c.1525–1535 by Giulio Romano. Not only did he work on the very building itself, Romano—a skilled designer and artist—worked hard and long at decorating the palatial interiors. He created illusions using form, texture and colour. Romano's many skills and incredible imagination led to the wonderful garden grottoes and mesmerising frescoes at the Palazzo del Te. Both the palace and its frescoes are important works of the Mannerist movement.

▲ *Wedding Banquet of Cupid and Psyche*, a fresco by Giulio Romano at Palazzo del Te

▲ Detail from the *Fall of the Giants* shows Romano's skill at turning a flat wall into a brilliant and turbulent 3D illusion

A Vista of Villas

Villas are grand country estates. They were first built as rambling homes for wealthy Romans in ancient times. The better-preserved ruins of such villas inspired Renaissance architects in the 15th and 16th centuries. This influence can be seen in the Villa Madama designed by Raphael. Ancient villas also influenced Pope Pius IV's Casino, built by Pirro Ligorio, in the Vatican gardens. However, Renaissance villas tried to be more symmetrical and less rambling. The first villas were built by the affluent Medici family. A symbol of power, villas were adorned with long colonnades, towers and gardens. Water features were incredibly popular and gardens featured fountains, reflecting pools and large reservoirs.

▲ Fontana dell'Ovato at the Villa d'Este

▲ Villa Barbaro, one of many iconic villas created by Andrea Palladio, is now a UNESCO World Heritage Site

▲ The magnificent Villa Aldobrandini, designed by Giacomo della Porta

Medici Villas

The Medici family constructed several villas in their home state of Tuscany. Many of these villas are now UNESCO World Heritage Sites. The villas were both leisure homes and palaces from which the Medicis ruled the land. One of the oldest is Cafaggiolo Castle. In 1443, Cosimo the Elder asked the architect Michelozzo to turn the castle into a villa. It is now a masterpiece of Renaissance architecture.

Equally old is the villa at Careggi. Like most Florentine villas, it is also a working farm. Michelozzo remodelled the fortified villa. He opened it up by building loggias. Those on the upper floor looked out over a walled garden full of myrtles, olives, oaks, poplars, pines and citrus trees. Other such early villas came about from the extensive rebuilding of older Medici castles.

▲ Medici Villa di Cafaggiolo

▶ A view of the Villa di Cafaggiolo painted by 16th-century Flemish artist Giusto Utens

▲ Villa Medici at Careggi

Villa Medici in Fiesole

Michelozzo built the Villa Medici in Fiesole from scratch. Thus, it has a stronger Renaissance character. The villa became a gathering place for artists and scholars. Michelozzo had followed Classical ideals in his design. The villa is a quadrangular building with square stone windows and broad loggias. Built over 1451–1457, this Medici villa has elegant terraces cut into a stony hillside. There are broad and amazing views of the River Arno and the city of Florence.

▶ Villa Medici at Fiesole

Villa d'Este

The fabulous Villa d'Este is an estate in Tivoli with Mannerist buildings, grand fountains and terraced gardens. The architect Pirro Ligorio created it for Cardinal Ippolito II d'Este. The villa is most famous for its mid-16th century gardens, set on a steep slope of the Sabine hills. A river plunges down the slope and its waters are channelled into a wonderful variety of fountains, including the remarkable 'water organ'. The stream runs around the garden ostentatiously creating a forceful, theatrical effect.

▲ Water rising from the Villa d'Este's Fountain of Neptune, with the famous water organ in the background

▲ Pegasus in the gardens of Villa d'Este

💡 Isn't It Amazing!

Ligorio's design for Villa d'Este was influenced by Roman ruins in Tivoli. The town of Tivoli had long been a popular summer residence due to its cool, high location and its closeness to the villa of the ancient Roman Emperor Hadrian I. In fact, statues dug up from the ancient villa ultimately decorated the gardens of the Cardinal's villa.

Secular Architecture

Renaissance architects aligned themselves with Humanism, in which humanity and individuality are of more importance than dogma and superstition. As a result, architects of the time had great civic pride. This led to the construction of many secular buildings for public prosperity. One of the first was Brunelleschi's Hospital of the Innocents, an orphanage, with its elegant colonnade linking the charitable home to the public square. Another was the Laurentian Library where scholars could consult the immense collection of books established by the Medici family. The spirit of individuality eventually led many Renaissance architects to Mannerism. This broke through the strict regularity and mathematical proportions of Roman times to more playful and exaggerated symmetries.

▲ Frescoes such as the 1610 Visit of Cosimo II de Medici in the Foundling Hospital by Bernardo Poccetti adorn the Renaissance orphanage Ospedale degli Innocenti (Hospital of the Innocents)

 ## Teatro Olimpico

Built by the genius Andrea Palladio, the Teatro Olimpico is the only surviving theatre of its time. It was also the first indoor theatre built using stone. This is because, during the Renaissance, a theatre was not a standalone building. It was more of a temporary arrangement in a courtyard or a hall. The Teatro Olimpico's design was based on the ancient Roman theatre at Orange, France. The stage is 25 metre across and 7 metre deep. It looks up to steep tiers of seats. Palladio's theatre sits inside a pre-existing hall. Although it is indoors, it creates the illusion of being outside! The ceiling is painted sky blue. Additionally, it has the most elaborate *scaenae frons*, which is the decorated and permanent background of a Roman theatre. It has five doors. Beyond the large central door are three different vistas of city streets. Behind the four other doors are forced perspective views of a city street.

▲ The stage at Teatro Olimpico; the scaenae frons beyond the central door was done in wood and plaster by the famous architect and stage designer Vincenzo Scamozzi (1552–1616)

▲ Teatro Olimpico with its statue-filled niches and blue sky ceiling

Bridge of Sighs

The Ponte dei Sospiri (Bridge of Sighs) is a landmark of Venice. It is an arched, fully enclosed structure of white limestone. Built in 1600, it runs over a narrow canal between the Doge's Palace and the prisons. Antonio Contino designed this bridge with a single arch and in Istrian stone. The two barred windows offered passing convicts their last look at the world before they were imprisoned. Their supposed sighs gave the bridge its name. The top of the bridge is decorated with scrolls. At the bottom, a series of stern faces look down on passing gondolas.

▲ Gondolas row past the grim heads of the Bridge of Sighs, Venice

Laurentian Library

In 1523, Michelangelo was asked to build a library for the Medicis' extensive collection of books and manuscripts. The resulting Laurentian Library sits on the third storey atop older monastic buildings. It is made up of a reading room and a vestibule (entrance hall). The vestibule is one of Michelangelo's great achievements. It is famous for a spectacular stairway whose design came to Michelangelo in a dream. At a time when architects followed rules of strict proportions, Michelangelo created powerful curved steps that poured down from the reading room. He even designed the carved benches in the library.

★ Incredible Individuals

Andrea Palladio (1508–1580) is possibly the most important 16th-century architect of northern Italy. His *palazzi* and villas, such as La Rotonda, and his *The Four Books of Architecture* influenced Western architects for centuries. It created a new style of architecture in later times called Palladianism in his honour.

▲ Statue of Andrea Palladio in Vicenza, Italy

▲ The staircase in the Laurentian Library

◀ Laurentian Library (Biblioteca Medicea Laurenziana) is a historical library in Florence, Italy. It was built in the cloister of the Basilica of San Lorenzo under the patronage of Pope Clement VII

Boboli Gardens

Located behind the fabulous Palazzo Pitti, the Boboli Gardens were created for the Medicis. Boboli is like a museum of multicoloured plants and amazing statues. The mixture of art and nature is characteristic of the Renaissance.

The Architects

Boboli Gardens were originally designed by Niccolò Tribolo. After his death, Bartolomeo Ammannati (1511–1592) took over and later Bernardo Buontalenti (1531–1608). Many other people helped complete the gardens including Davide Fortini and Giorgio Vasari. However, they all followed the original design.

▲ *Powerful sculptures overlook the city of Florence*

▲ *Green alley in Boboli Gardens, Florence*

The Amphitheatre

While designing the garden, Niccolò Tribolo thought to use the quarry at the base of the hill to build a great, horseshoe-shaped amphitheatre. This idea was brought to life after his death by several architects. In 1599, steps were added to it. Niches were built and filled with bronze statues and clay urns. Ancient Roman artefacts were added in later times. These include a granite basin from the Baths of Caracalla and an obelisk, which was brought from Egypt to Rome in 30 BC, and from Rome to Boboli in 1790.

▶ *A view of the amphitheatre from Palazzo Pitti*

Palazzo Pitti

In the mid-15th century, Florentine banker Luca Pitti constructed a palazzo by the River Arno. It was perhaps designed by Luca Fancelli for a project by Filippo Brunelleschi. After Pitti's death, the Medicis took over the unfinished palace. Cosimo I and his wife Eleonora charged Bartolomeo Ammannati with the task of converting it into a princely palace. Ammannati doubled its volume, added side wings and created a most awe-inspiring Renaissance palace.

▲ *The garden-facing facade of Palazzo Pitti with the Roman granite basin and Egyptian obelisk at the centre*

Grottoes

Mannerist gardens usually feature artificial grottoes. The wonderful Buontalenti Grotto lies opposite the entrance to Boboli. It has three linked chambers with stucco decorations and frescoes showing mythological tales. Most famous are the rural scenes painted by Bernardino Poccetti (1548–1612). Sculptor Vincenzo de' Rossi (1525–1587) added statues of the Trojan prince Paris kidnapping Helen, queen of Sparta. The third chamber holds a basin with the goddess Venus sculpted by Giambologna.

▲ *Part of the Buontalenti Grotto showing stucco work, frescoes and the statues of Paris and Helen*

Amazing Statues

A number of Giambologna's most important sculptures are found at the Boboli Gardens. The amazing Fountain of the Ocean is one of these. At its granite centre stands Neptune. He is surrounded by river gods representing the Nile, Ganges and Euphrates. The statue stands at the Isolotto, an islet laid out by Alfonso Parigi in the middle of a pond. Another fantastic sculpture is the Dwarf Morgante, a fat, nude dwarf riding a tortoise. It symbolises laziness and wisdom.

▶ *Statue of Andromeda at the Isolotta; in the background is the Fountain of the Ocean*

Religious Architecture

Over the 15th and 16th centuries, architects such as Bramante, Palladio, Antonio da Sangallo the Younger and Vincenzo Scamozzi showed a mastery over Classical styles. They revived these elements in churches and basilicas. Yet, they added their own personal inspiration to build never-before-seen structures. In the later days, their style became more ornamental. They incorporated statuary and decorative **cupolas**.

▲ Donato Bramante

▲ Andrea Palladio

▲ Antonio da Sangallo the Younger

▲ Vincenzo Scamozzi

Tempietto

In Rome, Bramante caught the eye of Cardinal Della Rovere, who later became Pope Julius II. For him, Bramante created one of the deeply harmonious *tempietto* (small chapel) of San Pietro in Montorio. The church was commissioned by Ferdinand and Isabella, rulers of Spain. It is believed that St Peter was crucified at this very spot. Built in 1502, the *tempietto* is a Classical circular building surrounded by columns. Bramante's dome, raised on slender columns, completes the sculpture-like temple.

Incredible Individuals

Donato Bramante (1444–1514) brought Early Renaissance to Milan and High Renaissance to Rome. He was more-or-less the court architect to Ludovico Sforza, the ruler of Milan. In this deeply Gothic town, Bramante built many churches in the Classical style. His greatest work here is perhaps the Santa Maria delle Grazie. However, Bramante's grandest contribution to Renaissance is undoubtedly St Peter's Basilica in Rome.

▲ A section of Santa Maria delle Grazie, Milan

◀ The tempietto of San Pietro in Montorio

Il Redentore

Located on the island of Giudecca in Venice, the 16th-century Chiesa del Santissimo Redentore (Church of the Most Holy Redeemer) is better known as Il Redentore. It was built to thank God for saving the city from a horrific outbreak of the plague. Designed by Andrea Palladio, the church sits beautifully on the waterfront. Its dazzling white facade stands under a large dome, which is topped by a statue of Christ the Redeemer. Inside the church is a series of interconnected spaces between the entrance and the high altar. Many important paintings decorate the building. This Renaissance masterpiece was only completed after Palladio's death. His foreman, Antonio da Ponte, faithfully followed the original designs.

▲ Il Redentore on the island of Giudecca, Venice

Basilica Palladiana

One of Palladio's important early works, the Palazzo delle Ragione was redesigned by Palladio with the use of loggias, and thus came to be known as Basilica Palladiana.. This Gothic original was decorated with red and yellow diamonds of Verona marble. This can still be seen behind Palladio's work. Palladio added his hallmark **serliana openings** to its white marble exterior. The ground floor is built in the Doric order. The upper floor is an enormous hall with Ionic supports. This is where the town's Grand Council met. The entire building is topped by a copper-lined roof like an inverted ship's hull.

▲ Basilica Palladiana with its serliana windows and peculiar roof

Church of San Giorgio Maggiore

Designed in 1566 by Palladio, the Church of San Giorgio Maggiore was finished in 1610 by the talented Vincenzo Scamozzi (1548–1616). The church dominates the island of San Giorgio Maggiore. Palladio's facade is typically Mannerist with Classical elements. This makes it look like an imposing ancient Roman temple with giant columns and triangular tops. On a sunny day, the spacious interior is filled with light. A screen of pillars separates the high altar from the choir beyond.

▶ Church of San Giorgio Maggiore

The Spread of Renaissance

During the 16th century, France and Spain rose to power. Other European countries began to compete for power too. These included the Low Countries (modern-day Belgium, Luxembourg and the Netherlands), England, Germany and Russia. The Renaissance spirit was fully formed by this time. At the height of its glory, it found its way to various courts across Europe. However, in each country, the Classical style of architecture was adapted to suit local tastes and traditions. It is not always clear what buildings qualify as Renaissance. Many are more easily classified as Mannerist buildings. Indeed, it can be difficult to clearly see the start, the end or the influence of Renaissance architecture in many European nations.

▲ Inigo Jones's arcaded central square at Covent Garden, London, was inspired by Renaissance piazzas (town squares) of Venice and Florence

▲ The City Hall at Delft is a Mannerist building. It was built in 1618–1620 by Hendrick de Keyser, who helped establish the Dutch Renaissance style

Spain & Portugal

Spanish and Portuguese Renaissance follow similar paths. In Spain, this period can be divided into three phases. Its early Renaissance architecture is called Plateresque. This began in the late 15th century and lasted till about 1560. The period 1525–1560 showed a true adoption of Classical styles. The last phase, from 1560 to the end of the 16th century, is called Herreran. It is named after Juan de Herrera, the most important Spanish architect of the time. The buildings of this period are severe looking.

▲ The severe, grey domes of the San Lorenzo de El Escorial, Spain, is characteristic of the Herreran style of architecture

Manueline Architecture

In Portugal, the architecture of the late 15th and early 16th centuries is called Manueline. It is named after the ruling king of the period, Manuel I. The style is very decorative and not truly Classical. Instead, it uses small Classical motifs as ornaments on Gothic-style buildings. The abundance of decorations reflects the wealth of maritime Portugal. Towards the end of the 16th century, architect Filippo Terzi created austere buildings in Portugal, such as the church of São Vicente de Fora in Lisbon. These were similar to Herrera's style.

▲ Belém Tower in Lisbon shows Renaissance motifs incorporated into the grand Manueline style

Convent of Christ, Tomar

After the mid-16th century, Portugal saw a truly Classical style. This can be seen in the work of the talented Diogo de Torralva at the cloister of the Convent of Christ (1557–1562). Located in the town of Tomar, its rhythmic bays show alternating arches and Classical columns. The mix of Doric and Ionic orders is similar to the Italian High Renaissance.

▲ The cloister of John III at the Convent of Christ, Tomar

In Real Life

The intelligent and cultured King Francis I invited Leonardo da Vinci to France. Da Vinci came with his artworks, many of which remained in the country. Even today, France has the largest collection of the master's paintings. This includes the famous *Mona Lisa*, known as *La Joconde* in France.

▶ *Statue of Leonardo da Vinci in Milan, Italy*

France

The French Renaissance is best seen in its 16th-century *châteaus* (country mansions). The earliest influence of the period is seen in Loire Valley's Château d'Amboise. During the Renaissance, on the orders of Charles VII, Louis XII, and Francis I, the château was refurnished. Renaissance blossomed under Francis I. It developed into French Mannerism, also called Henry II style.

▼ *The domed Château de Chantilly is representative of Henry II style, a type of Northern Mannerism that dominated France over the 16th century*

Renaissance Architecture in France

▲ Château d'Azay-le-Rideau in the Loire Valley

Over 1494–1525, France launched many invasions against Italy. Thus, French kings and aristocrats came under the spell of the Renaissance. For 25 years, during the reigns of Louis XII (1462–1515) and Francis I (1494–1547), the French owned Milan. This was the capital city of Lombardy in northern Italy. It was thus the Lombard Renaissance style that first appeared in France. Early French Renaissance was followed by a Mannerist period that dominated France till the end of the 16th century.

 ## Château de Chenonceau

▲ The medieval Château d'Ussé with its Renaissance courtyard is said to have inspired the castle in Charles Perrault's fairy tale, Sleeping Beauty

Possibly the first French architect to gain a universal outlook on architecture like the Italians was Philibert de l'Orme (c. 1510–1570). He added a graceful Renaissance touch to the older, medieval Château de Chenonceau. He built a five-arched bridge to connect the château on the north bank of the river to the south bank.

◀ The Renaissance bridge of the Château de Chenonceau

A Noble Style

Most middle-class families continued to patronise their home-grown Gothic style. It was the aristocracy that adopted the new Classical style. During the time of Louis XII and the early reign of Francis I, the French capital lay in Tours, near the Loire Valley. Thus, the towns in the valley were the earliest to express Classical architecture. This can be seen today in the châteaus of Amboise and Blois. In many cases, the new buildings, gardens and courtyards were added to older medieval castles.

▲ At the Gothic Château de Blois, the wing of Francis I was built over 1515–1524 and shows greater influence of Classical Italian styles

Château de Chambord

The largest early French Renaissance building is the hunting lodge built from 1519 for Francis I at Chambord. The vast château is 156 metre long with a rectangular court. The surrounding wall has round towers at the corners. The genius of Leonardo da Vinci can be seen in the château, in the central staircase and the inventive ventilation system. He had been invited to France by Francis I, who admired him. To cap it all, the château is fortified and protected by a moat. It is set in a garden surrounded by a 32-km-long wall.

▶ Frenchman Pierre Lescot (c. 1500–1578) established the grand Mannerist French Renaissance style, best seen in the rebuilding of the Louvre Palace that he did for Francis I

◀ Château de Chambord

Dutch and Flemish Renaissance

The area occupied by modern-day Belgium, Luxembourg and the Netherlands is historically called the Low Countries. The Flemish and Dutch people of this region had Gothic preferences until the 17th century. At most, Classical motifs—similar to those in France—were added on as decorations to Gothic buildings. These can be seen in some 16th-century buildings in Flanders (northern Belgium), which had strong trade relations with the rest of Europe. In the early 17th century, Dutch sculptor and architect Hendrick de Keyser developed the Renaissance style in the Netherlands. His wonderful Mannerist creations were so unique that he was made the municipal architect of Amsterdam. Another important figure was Hans Vredeman de Vries who became famous as a garden architect.

▲ Designed by Gothic architect Rombout Keldermans, the Palace of Margaret of Austria showcases formal Renaissance motifs

Architects

Some of the earliest and most notable architects who took inspiration from Classicism were Lieven de Key (1560–1627), Hendrick de Keyser (1565–1621) and Cornelis Danckerts de Ry (1561–1634). Lieven de Key is most famous for building Haarlem's Meat Market. As the 17th century progressed, people began to look for purer Renaissance forms. Among the architects who developed the new style were the celebrated Jacob van Campen (1596–1657), Philips Vingboons (1607–1678) and Pieter Post (1608–1669). The gigantic Town Hall of Amsterdam constructed over 1648–1655, is one of van Campen's masterworks. It was converted into the royal palace in 1806 when Napoleon Bonaparte set his brother upon the Dutch throne.

▲ The Town Hall of Amsterdam features sculptures in the style of Dutch Classicism symbolising justice and commerce

▲ Originally built around 1633–1644 as a residence for Count Johan Maurits van Nassau-Siegen, the Mauritshuis was designed by Jacob van Campen and built by Pieter Post in the Dutch Classical style

In Real Life

Built over 1602–1603 by Lieven de Key using costly materials, the beautiful Vleeshal (literally, meat hall) was the only place in Haarlem allowed to sell fresh meat until 19th century!

RENAISSANCE ARCHITECTURE 25

Stadhuis

The most eye-catching building of the Flemish Renaissance is the Stadhuis (Town Hall) of Antwerp. It was designed by Flemish architect Loys du Foys and Italian architect Nicolo Scarini and executed by Cornelis Floris II over 1561–1565. The building replaced Antwerp's smaller medieval town hall to show the city's prosperity as a trade port. The town hall follows the stern repeating symmetry common in Classical architecture. It is softened by a wealth of detail unique to the Low Countries. Doric and Ionic **pilasters** separate the large windows.

▲ The Town Hall at Antwerp

Isn't It Amazing!

Classical caryatids are stone carvings of draped women. Hans Vredeman de Vries's imaginative caryatids from c. 1565 show how such Classical motifs changed in the Low Countries.

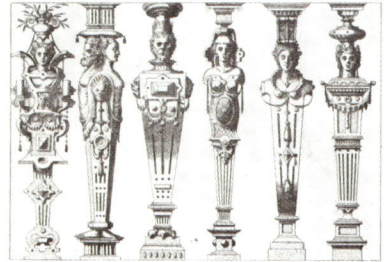

▲ Hans Vredeman de Vries's angular caryatids from his architectural drawings

Grand Place

Guilds are formed when professionals come together in groups to oversee practice and fair play in their trade. They are formed by artisans or merchants, for instance. In the Low Countries, many guilds from the 15th and 16th centuries were wealthy and powerful. They built guild houses and private homes that reflected the incoming architectural styles from Italy—or what they understood of it. The grand town square of the bustling city of Brussels is surrounded by such buildings. Unlike the stern Classical Italian buildings though, the houses around the Grand Place are showy and opulent. They are ornamented with extravagant statues and motifs that include phoenixes, horses, scrolls, urns, fluted pillars and lace-like details.

▲ Grand Place (central square) is adorned every other year with thousands of begonias for the Brussels Flower Carpet event

▲ Roman statuary and roundels adorning the showy facade of La Louve, the house of the guild of archers, at Grand Place

The Iberian Peninsula

The southwest corner of Europe is a large peninsula called Iberia. It is mostly taken up by the countries of Spain and Portugal. During the Middle Ages, it was inhabited by Islamic citizens of Arab, Spanish and North African origins. The Catholic kingdoms called them the Moors and drove them out of Spain by 1492. However, the newly Catholic peninsula admired the Moorish architecture left behind. When the Italian Renaissance entered Spain and Portugal, it could not completely dislodge this inheritance.

▲ *The Alcázar of Toledo, was originally a Roman palace. Its facade and courtyard were rebuilt in the Renaissance style by Spanish architect Alonso de Covarrubias (1488–1570)*

Plateresque Spain

From the Catholic occupation of Spain in 1492 till about 1560, Spanish architecture went through a phase called Plateresque. There was no real change in the proportions or designs of buildings. Instead, Italian artisans who came over to create tombs or altars introduced Renaissance terms to the Spaniards. Spanish architects experimented with decorative pilasters and arabesques. However, the splendour-loving culture of Spain was markedly different from the stern Classicism of Renaissance Italy. Thus, the changes were purely ornamental.

▲ *The Royal Hospital at Santiago de Compostela was built over 1501–1511 by Enrique de Egas. Its ornamented facade is interspersed with large expanses of bare wall*

The Town Hall of Seville

The construction for the outstanding Ayuntamiento (Town Hall) of Seville was started in 1527 by Diego de Riaño. The building shows the influence of Lombard Renaissance in its panelled pilasters and relief-covered half-columns. Numerous medallions lie on the walls, under the windows and between the pilasters.

◀ *The Plateresque facade of Seville's Town Hall*

RENAISSANCE ARCHITECTURE

Renaissance Portugal

The reign of Manuel I (1469–1521) was a time of great wealth for Portugal. As most of these riches came from sea trade, Manueline decorations were naturally ocean-themed. Coral motifs, barnacle-encrusted mouldings and carvings of seaweed and algae were popular. Anchors, stone ropes and seafaring instruments were seen over windows and doors. This unique style existed between the Gothic and Renaissance phases in Portugal.

Classical Period

The Classical style first appeared in Portugal in 1526 in the Palace of Charles V within the complex of the amazing Alhambra, the magnificent Moorish palace-fortress. It was designed by Pedro Machuca, a Spaniard who had studied in Italy. As Holy Roman Emperor, Charles V dominated European politics. His palace was to be a statement of his power. However, the palace was never completed. It is a square building with a circular courtyard that is 30 metre in diameter. The arena is surrounded by a colonnade with austere Doric and Ionic columns. The plan is thus truly Classical with the correct harmony of proportions.

▲ A window at the Convent of Christ in Tomar showcases Manueline decorations

▲ The central courtyard of the Palace of Charles V was intended for bullfights and tournaments

Herreran Architecture

The culmination of Spanish Renaissance occurred with the Herreran style. It is named after Juan de Herrera (c. 1530–1597), the architect of Imperial Spain in the 16th century. The finest example of his work is the El Escorial palace built for Philip II, the son of Charles V. While the father brought Renaissance to Spain, the son promoted more Mannerist creations. Herreran architecture enforced geometrical principals and clean spaces. Decorations were kept to a minimum.

Isn't It Amazing!

Some of the best examples of Plateresque style can be seen in the historic town of Salamanca. The Monterrey Palace, built in 1539 by Rodrigo Gil de Hontañon and Martìn de Santiago, even inspired architects of the 19th and early 20th centuries! The Convento de las Dueñas and the Casa de las Muertes (House of the Dead) are two other Plateresque gems.

▲ Hans Vredeman de Vries's angular caryatids from his architectural drawings

◀ The Collegiate Church of San Pedro, Lerma, exemplifies the clean-cut facade of the Herreran style

El Escorial

The Royal Monastery of San Lorenzo de El Escorial was built by King Philip II of Spain. The complex holds a royal palace and a vast monastery. Rising from the foothills of the Sierra de Guadarrama mountains, the complex is a massive rectangle measuring 206 metre by 161 metre. The devout Philip II established a basilica at its centre. This is one of the few religious structures outside Italy to use the Classical style of architecture. Construction began in 1563 under the Spanish Renaissance architect Juan Bautista de Toledo. He is thought to be responsible for its plans, style and the execution of El Escorial. After his death in 1567, his assistant Juan de Herrera took over and made many alterations.

Philip's Necropolis

El Escorial was constructed on the site of an older monastery. Philip II wanted a place where all the Spanish rulers could be buried. He thus actively took part in the planning of the complex. In particular, the king removed anything that seemed decorative or showy. El Escorial is thus a massive, forbidding structure with plain walls and seemingly endless rows of windows. The austere facade is constructed entirely of grey granite. The interior is equally severe and lacking in decoration. A few Classical touches are seen in the use of Doric columns and plain arches.

▲ The Courtyard of the Kings and an entrance to the basilica

Incredible Individuals

During the 1557 Battle of Saint Quentin, the Spanish army is said to have destroyed a church dedicated to St Lawrence. Philip II supposedly dedicated the monastery at El Escorial to St Lawrence to atone for the destruction.

▼ The vast and serene monastery at El Escorial

RENAISSANCE ARCHITECTURE

The Layout

Juan de Toledo's ambitious design for this part-royal court, part-monastic construction took form in over a year. His ground plan is thought to represent the grid of hot coals on which Saint Lawrence was martyred. The royal gardens lie to the east and the monastery gardens to the south. The outer buildings form a perfect square and are four stories high with square towers at the corners. They enclose the inner complex like a fortress. Beyond the central church runs the monastery's **cloister**, which encloses the Courtyard of the Evangelists, one of Herrera's fine creations.

▲ Western facade showing the main entrance to the basilica and the monastery's front yard

The Church

The Courtyard of the Kings opens beyond the main entrance. It is dominated by the central structure, which is the basilica. This serene building is topped by a massive cupola that was inspired by Michelangelo's dome for St Peter's Basilica in Rome. Two striking bell towers rise cleanly on either side.

▶ The high altar inside the basilica is supported by Ionic columns

Isn't It Amazing!

Philip II founded the library at El Escorial. The room, with its marble floors, beautiful wooden shelves and amazing painted ceiling, is home to more than 4,700 rare manuscripts—including **illuminated manuscripts**. There are also some 40,000 printed books in the collection.

▲ The El Escorial library

The Monastery

Toledo's monastery was a great rectangle made of three parts. On the south were five cloisters, which included the palace and offices. The monks' living quarters lay in the north.

▶ El Escorial, home of the kings of Spain

The British Isles

During the 15th and 16th centuries, England was largely on bad terms with the Pope and the Holy Roman Emperor. First, Henry VIII of England broke away from the Catholic Church and set himself up as the head of the Protestant English Church. Later, his daughter Queen Elizabeth I went to war with Philip II of Spain, a devout and powerful Catholic monarch. As a result, there is little true Renaissance architecture in England. Instead, the evolving styles of this period are named after the rulers—Tudor style (after the house of Henry VIII), Elizabethan style and Jacobean style (after James I of England).

▲ Hatfield House is a grand Jacobean country house set in formal gardens

Identifying the Styles

The Tudor style used Renaissance decorations on native Gothic designs. Such adornments included low arches, rows of rectangular windows and patterned brickwork. This is mostly seen in secular buildings such as the Hampton Court Palace. In Elizabethan times, the houses changed into tall, rectangular buildings. Windows became mullioned and used a great deal of glass. The Jacobean age saw the style becoming more consistent and formal. The buildings included Classical columns and arched galleries, though still adorned with fanciful details. Throughout the Renaissance period, English courtiers built prodigy houses. These were showy country mansions meant to attract visits from the reigning king and queen.

Incredible Individuals

Towards the end of Queen Elizabeth's rule, the painter and architect Inigo Jones (1573–1652) brought real Renaissance designs to England. His bold work with Classical proportions and detail was inspired by the theories of Andrea Palladio. The Banqueting House at Whitehall is one of his few remaining masterworks.

▶ Inigo Jones

▲ Decorative Tudor brickwork on the chimneys of Hampton Court

▶ Bess of Hardwick, the richest woman in Elizabethan times, built her house with such massive windows that it led to the popular rhyme, 'Hardwick Hall, more glass than wall'. Glass was indeed a luxury during this period

Hampton Court

The unintentional symmetry of Hampton Court makes it appear more Classical than Gothic. The palace was constructed by Cardinal Wolsey in 1515 and later taken over by Henry VIII. Its Renaissance elements are largely decorative. For instance, a number of terracotta roundels by the Italian sculptor Giovanni da Maiano adorn the gateways.

Longleat

Built by the statesman Sir John Thynne (1515–1580), Longleat is one of Elizabethan England's finest **prodigy houses**. It was constructed with the help of Robert Smythson, a leading architect of the time, and a number of other designers. The building was arranged symmetrically around two courts. The third story was most likely added after Thynne's death. The three stories follow the Classic orders of Doric, Ionic and Corinthian style.

▲ Bust of Roman Emperor Tiberius decorating Hampton Court

▲ Longleat House

Wollaton Hall

One of Robert Smythson's most amazing buildings, the symmetrical Wollaton Hall is basically square with square towers at four corners. The great hall lies at the centre and rises above the rest of the building. Despite this basic plan, the house looks sensational with its mullioned windows, arched niches, columns and many Classical touches. The playful exaggerations are similar to Italian Mannerism. The corner towers are decorated with Flemish strapwork, which are raised and curved bands that look like leather straps.

▲ Wollaton Hall

Word Check

Apse: It is a semi-circular room-like space that is covered with a hemispherical dome.

Bays: It is the space distinguished by vertical lines or planes, i.e. elements like columns.

Blind arches: It is an arch decorating a solid wall, instead of opening into a window or passage.

Burghers: They were the privileged citizens of European towns who were often elected to some governing role.

Cloister: It is a covered walkway, usually in the form of a quadrangle, along the wall of a convent, college or monastery.

Cupola: It is a rounded dome that forms the ceiling of a building.

Garrison: It is a body of troops stationed in a particular location.

High Renaissance: It is the period when the Renaissance influence was at its highest point.

Illuminated manuscripts: They are medieval texts with miniature paintings and decorations in gold or silver.

Loggia: It is a gallery or room with open sides that looks out onto a garden or some other scenery.

Pilaster: A rectangular column that projects from the wall

Prodigy houses: Showy mansions built during the Elizabethan and Jacobean era

Relief: They are carvings that are raised from a solid surface, like a wall.

Renaissance: It is the period between the 15th and 17th century in Europe when there was a surge in the rediscovery of art, architecture, literature and philosophy.

Roundels: It is a small disc or decorative medallion.

Serliana openings: It is also called a Palladian or Venetian window; a three-part window made of a large, arched central section bordered by two narrower sections having square tops.